HOLLYWOOD
MUSICALS

HOLLYWOOD MUSICALS

Julie Koerner

FRIEDMAN/FAIRFAX
PUBLISHERS

A FRIEDMAN/FAIRFAX BOOK

© 1993, 1997 Michael Friedman Publishing Group, Inc.

Library of Congress Cataloging-in-Publication number 95-137492

ISBN 1-56799-354-0

Editor: Nathaniel Marunas
Art Director: Jeff Batzli
Designer: Lynne Yeamans
Photography Editor: Jennifer Crowe McMichael

Grateful acknowledgment is given to authors, publishers, and photographers, for permission to reprint material. Every effort has been made to determine copyright owners of photographs and illustration. In the case of any omissions, the publishers will be pleased to make suitable acknowledgments in future editions.

Color separations by Ocean Graphic International Company Ltd.
Printed in Singapore by KHL Printing Co. Pte Ltd.

10 9 8 7 6 5 4 3 2 1

For bulk purchases and special sales, please contact:
Friedman/Fairfax Publishers
Attention: Sales Department
15 West 26th Street
New York, NY 10010
(212) 685-6610 FAX (212) 685-1307
Visit our website: http://www.metrobooks.com

CONTENTS

Introduction

I n the beginning there was light. Electric light. The concept of motion pictures was

born with the advent of Edison's light bulb, at the onset of the era of invention.

One of many revolutionary electrical devices invented by the "Wizard of Menlo

Park," the light bulb was the foundation for what is now the bountiful, prosperous,

global industry of moviemaking. From their simple roots as ghostly, flickering diver-

sions, movies have become a powerful branch of the mass media and an internationally

appreciated art form. In the short span of one hundred years, nurtured by artistry and

technology, movies have grown from brief, silent, slapstick novelties into potent vehicles

for powerful artistic expression, sophisticated and lavish entertainment, poignant social

commentary, and perhaps most significantly, celluloid mirrors that reflect the life and

times of the societies in which they are made.

Thomas Alva Edison, inventor of the phonograph in 1877 and the light bulb in 1879, is often credited with inventing motion pictures. But a closer look at their development reveals that quite a few other people also had significant roles in creating the phenomenon that has come to be known as the movies.

Pictures

Still photography, the precursor of moving pictures, was perfected by the French artist Louis-Jacques-Mandé Daguerre (1789–1851), who made the first photographs in 1837. His "daguerreotypes" were complicated creations in which the "film" was actually a silver plate coated

Thomas Alva Edison poses with his revolutionary invention, the phonograph.

An engraving of Daguerre mixing chemicals in his laboratory.

with iodine. After an exposure was made, processing was done painstakingly, by exposing the plate to mercury vapor. Since the silver plate was not nearly as sensitive to light as is present-day film, Daguerre's subjects were often required to pose like statues for fifteen, twenty, and sometimes thirty minutes to successfully complete an exposure.

Daguerre's innovation fired the imaginations of other inventors who were fascinated by the prospect of capturing,

immortalizing, and reproducing brief moments of "real life." A variety of methods and techniques were developed to accomplish this during the second half of the nineteenth century, but it wasn't until the late 1800s that U.S. inventor George Eastman (1854–1932) came up with a celluloid-based film, a breakthrough that would eventually provide a suitable medium for moving pictures.

Daguerre showed the way and Eastman provided the means, but quite a lot of light passed through the lens before Edison put it all together.

A Day at the Races

Early attempts at "motion pictures" were not very successful because of the obvious limitations of the only applicable tool available at the time: the still camera. But ingenuity prevailed, and "movies" were born when English photographer Eadweard Muybridge (1830–1904) was able to convincingly show movement on film.

The unlikely inspiration for Muybridge's accomplishment was a bet made by California's horse-training governor, Leland Stanford. Stanford enlisted Muybridge's help in proving something that could not be seen with the naked eye: that a horse becomes momentarily airborne when it is running. To win the bet, Stanford had to prove that at some moment during each stride, all four of a running horse's hooves leave the ground simultaneously.

To test the theory, Muybridge positioned first twelve, then twenty-four, and finally forty-eight still cameras at spaced intervals around a track, each with a string attached to a raised shutter. As the horse ran past each camera, it tripped the shutter strings in turn, snapping a succession of pictures. The photographs showed a sequence of action that included a moment when all four hooves were off the ground, and Leland Stanford won his $25,000 bet (it was rumored that it cost him $40,000 to prove his assertion).

Right: This engraving shows Muybridge presenting his photographs at the Royal Academy. Below: Eadweard Muybridge's sequence of photographs capturing a horse in motion proved that the animal becomes airborne while galloping.

The Kinetograph, the Kinetoscope, and the Nickelodeon

Thomas Edison didn't seem very enthusiastic about moving pictures, except perhaps as accompaniment for the sounds made on his phonographs. But people all over the world were working on ways to record moving pictures, and because of his stature as the reigning genius of modern invention, many sent him their ideas, prototypes, and experiments. Some theorists insist that Edison usurped the design for the first motion picture camera, possibly from British inventor William Friese-Greene (1855–1921). Other historians believe that the first camera and viewer were built by an employee of Edison's named William Kennedy Laurie Dickson (1860–1932). Even the most ardent Edison disciple will agree that the development of his movie camera was a collaborative effort. Regardless, in 1891, Edison applied for patents on a camera, which he called a Kinetograph, and a viewer, which he called a Kinetoscope. The patents were issued in 1893, and Edison publicly displayed the inventions at the 1893 Columbian Exposition of the Chicago World's Fair, showing a film made by

Right: About thirty seconds of film wound around spools inside the Kinetoscope made it possible to repeat the reel over and over. Below: A kinetograph records action while a phonograph records sound separately.

Dickson. Perhaps the earliest film on record was also made by Dickson; it starred an Edison laboratory colleague named Fred Ott who could make himself sneeze at will. It was imaginatively titled *Fred Ott's Sneeze.*

Before long, Edison's kinetoscopes lined amusement halls and penny arcades, also known as peep shows and kinetoscope parlors. In order to see a minute of Fatima, the dancing Egyptian lady, the viewer put a penny in the slot, peered into an opening, and turned a crank to roll the film. By 1902 the films had been lengthened to almost ten minutes and the viewing machines were upgraded. The price was upgraded, too (to a nickel), thus creating the nickelodeon, which grew quickly in popularity.

Over the next ten years, more than five thousand nickelodeons opened in the United States. By buying nickelodeon machines, any ambitious entrepreneur could convert an amusement hall, dance parlor, vaudeville theater, or even a warehouse into a profitable enterprise with very low overhead. The public clamored for all kinds of movies; in response, Muybridge, Dickson, and other photographers filmed practically anything of interest, such as current vaudeville acts, clowns, jugglers,

Thomas Edison (1847–1931)

Thomas Alva Edison invented his first gadget when he was sixteen. He was given a job with the Grand Trunk Railway in Ontario,Canada, reporting hourly by telegraph to Toronto. He soon found it tedious, so he rigged a gadget between the clock and the transmitter that would automatically send the hourly message. That way he could sleep. From then on, Edison devoted his energies to inventing or improving on the inventions of others. He perfected a vote-recording machine and a stockticker, a telegraphic device that reported gold prices to stock brokers, and made major contributions toward the perfection of the telephone, the mimeograph machine, the typewriter, and the electric generator.

The invention of the "talking machine," or phonograph, in 1877, was one of Edison's most significant as it signaled a true breakthrough from its parent, the telegraph. Although other inventors had been working on providing electric light, it was Edison (and Sir Joseph William Swan) who discovered that a carbon filament enclosed inside an evacuated glass bulb would glow when heated electrically. This discovery eventually led to the development of the light bulb as we know it today.

By 1889, many inventors had been working on perfecting the motion picture camera, and once Edison turned his attention in that direction, progress was hastened. Even though he considered his phonograph the greater invention, and perceived moving pictures as novelty items, Edison threw his support behind his employee William Kennedy Laurie Dickson by appointing Dickson director of motion picture development. With Edison's clout, Dickson's perserverance, and George Eastman's celluloid paper, the Kinetograph and the Kinetoscope were born.

Despite early attempts by Dickson and others to convince Edison to build a projection screen, he balked at the idea. He insisted on sticking with the single-person viewer, the kinetoscope, probably for two reasons: he felt the picture was clearer and more precise, and Edison was never one to overlook profit. He felt the greater profit came in requiring people to view films individually rather than in groups. It was only after Thomas Armat invented the projector and proved its merit that Edison entered into a business agreement with him to patent and market the Vitascope. To be sure, Edison consistently underestimated the appeal of motion pictures. He was so sure the gimmick would not catch on that he didn't bother to spend the additional 150 dollars to apply for foreign patents on his inventions.

Edison and Dickson made major contributions to the film industry; besides the Kinetoscope and Kinetograph they perfected the use of perforated holes on each side of the film to hold it in position inside the camera, and they built the first film studio: a small room covered with black tar paper to keep light out. Inside Black Maria, as the studio was called, they cranked out films to be shown in Kinetoscope arcades across the country.

Left: The original Edison phonograph, an invention that changed the world. Below: Thomas Edison poses with the speaking phonograph at the National Academy of Sciences in 1878.

wrestlers, nude women, men and women dancing together, and natural scenes such as waves breaking or birds in flight.

The first nickelodeon films were designed to appeal to a mostly male mass audience. Films were often accompanied by live organ or piano music, and sometimes by a narrator who provided a plot line. With those embellishments, a ten-minute movie might be stretched to an hour-long presentation. Efforts were made to attract a wider audience to the nickelodeon parlors, but the entertainment was still considered too crude to appeal to a female audience, or to be considered suitable for young people.

The Big Picture

Thomas Edison seemed to consider his kinetoscope little more than a toy, but other inventors in the United States and Europe soon grasped the commercial potential of a slightly different device: a movie projector that would permit groups of people to simultaneously view a larger picture.

Two French brothers, Auguste and Louis Lumière, developed a portable camera and used 35mm film to make their first movie, *Workers Leaving the Lumière Factory*. The Lumières projected this and other films in Paris on December 28, 1895. At about the same time, Thomas Armat (1866–1948) invented a projector in the United States. He took his invention to Thomas Edison, and the two men formed a business partnership. Edison named the projector the Vitascope, and in 1896 sold it as his own, giving a share of the profits to Armat. (A few years later, Armat sued Edison for breaching this agreement by manufacturing a similar projector and keeping all the profits.)

As filmmaking equipment advanced technologically, filmmakers themselves became increasingly sophisticated. In France, a skilled magician bought a camera from the Lumière brothers and applied his technical and artistic talent to moviemaking. Georges Melies began to experiment in storytelling with his films

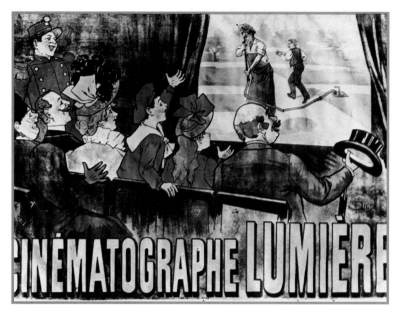

This promotional poster shows an audience laughing at the Lumières' Watering the Gardener.

Cinderella, The Dreyfus Affair, and *The Execution of Mary, Queen of Scots.* Contributions made by Melies affected moviemaking on both sides of the ocean, especially in Thomas Edison's film laboratories, where a young cameraman named Edwin S. Porter began to make films of his own. By 1903 Porter had made *The Life of an American Fireman* and a film that is still studied in film classes today, *The Great Train Robbery.*

Hollywood on the Hudson

Soon after Edwin S. Porter became head of production at the Edison studios, a young playwright by the name of David Wark Griffith (1875–1948) brought Porter one of his plays that had met with little success

The Lumières' *Watering the Gardener* (1895)

The father of Auguste (1862–1954) and Louis (1864–1948) Lumière was a photographer who built his own photographic plate factory in Lyons, France, then converted it so that it could be used to make celluloid film. The Lumière brothers were always experimenting with photography and equipment, and by 1895 they had transformed Edison's Kinetoscope and Kinetograph into a portable, "all in one" machine that photographed, developed, and projected its film. With this invention, they used 35mm film and determined the most effective film recording speed to be sixteen frames per second, both conventions that are still used today. And, before their other interests diverted them, they named their camera *Cinématographe*, the word from

The Lumières' Cinematographic Theater in Paris, where people got an early taste of moving pictures.

which many filmmaking terms are derived.

One of the films made by the Lumière brothers, *Watering the Gardener*, is an early example of what would come to be called slapstick comedy. The stationary camera, set up outdoors, shows a man watering a lawn with a garden hose while a little boy comes up behind him and steps on the hose, stopping the flow of water. The man turns the hose to his face to take a look inside, the boy lifts up his foot, and the water gushes out, directly into the man's face. The gardener chases the boy, catches him, spanks him, then goes back to his gardening. Physical comedy on film was born when this cause-and-effect story made its first audience laugh out loud.

on the stage. Unimpressed by the script, Porter hired Griffith as an actor rather than a writer. But Griffith turned out to be a mediocre actor during his brief stint with Edison; he soon moved over to Biograph, a studio trying to accelerate film production in order to meet the demands of the multiplying nickelodeon audiences.

Soon after joining Biograph, Griffith was asked to fill in for an absentee director. He wasn't fully aware of his directorial interest or talent until he teamed with cinematographer G.W. "Billy" Bitzer (1872–1944), and tried his hand at directing *The Adventures of Dollie*, about a baby kidnapped by a gypsy, then abandoned to fall in a stream, where she is rescued by a little boy and reunited with her family. While *Dollie* wasn't hailed as a masterpiece, it whetted Griffith's directorial appetite, and together with Bitzer, he spent the next ten years changing the course of movie history with inventive directorial achievements.

Georges Melies' background as a magician is evident in these whimsical stills from The Man with the Rubber Head.

Georges Melies (1861–1938)

Georges Melies, owner and proprietor of the Théâtre Robert-Houdin in France, was a magician and technician who became interested in working with movie cameras and soon became one of the world's most innovative and influential filmmakers. He founded the Star Film Company in 1896, and made more than five hundred movies in less than twenty years, including *The Conjuror, The Dreyfus Affair* (1899), *The Execution of Mary, Queen of Scots, The Magic Lantern,* and the fantasy *A Trip to the Moon* (1902).

Inspired no doubt by his background as a magician, Melies turned the camera into a magician's tool: he made subjects disappear and reappear by turning the camera off and on during movement, a technique now called "stop action." Melies was the first to use photographic tricks such as superimposition, which results in double exposures, the first to use slow motion and fast motion, the first to diffuse lighting to create fades and dissolves, and the first to direct lighting onto a scene from the sides rather than from the top of the set. In his filmic fairy tale *Cinderella* (1902), Melies became the first filmmaker to show a story with a beginning, middle, and end.

Melies' A Trip to the Moon is widely considered to be the first science-fiction film ever made.

Griffith was greatly responsible for expanding the brief, ten-minute shorts into feature-length films. Initially, it was tough to convince the producers that an audience would pay attention to a movie that ran longer than one reel, usually ten to twenty minutes. Griffith persevered, however, and following the lead of European directors who were already successfully showing longer movies, he made *Enoch Arden* (1911) in two reels. To his chagrin, Biograph insisted on showing the film only one reel at a time, until audiences demanded to see the entire movie at once, proving Griffith correct in his instincts. In fact, one of Griffith's greatest moviemaking talents was his instinctive ability to understand audiences and to make feature movies that were commercially viable. During the first decades of the 1900s, Griffith made a wide variety of movies, including *A Corner in Wheat*, *The*

Griffith on location filming Hearts of the World, *which was shot in England and France, about a tiny French village ravaged by war.*

Drunkard's Reformation, *Birth of a Nation*, and *Intolerance*.

Lured by promotions from the Los Angeles Chamber of Commerce, D.W. Griffith moved from Mamaroneck, New

Porter's *Life of an American Fireman* (1903) and *The Great Train Robbery* (1903)

In 1903 Edwin S. Porter (1870–1941) made a film about popular heroes of the era entitled *Life of an American Fireman*. He employed techniques for the first time that are still used in filmmaking today, most notably the use of a variety of camera angles to enhance the drama (a device now known as "point of view"). In the United States, *Life of an American Fireman* also introduced the concept of "screen narrative," a sophisticated way of advancing a story through emotion and reason, rather than by consecutive frame-by-frame storytelling.

The film begins with a fireman in his office falling asleep and having a dream, which appears in a super-imposed image above his head. In the dream, he sees a woman and child (some think the woman is his wife) who are in danger. This was the first time a movie audience could see what someone was thinking. He awakens, startled or frightened, and the next shot is a close-up of a hand triggering a fire alarm—the first use of that kind of dramatic camera angle. In the following scene, firemen scramble off their cots and scurry down the firepole. They leap onto fire engines that are hitched up to horses. The engines are seen moving quickly down the street, but close examination reveals that the engines are different from the ones seen in the interior shot, and the street is also different. Porter had used preexisting, or "stock," footage for the sequence, splicing it into the narrative—another first.

The rescue itself is shown from two different perspectives, inside and out. The woman and child are seen waiting to be rescued, and the firemen are shown raising a ladder to the window of the

Robbers enter the telegraph office in Porter's The Great Train Robbery.

In one of the scenes, the engineer is forced at gunpoint to detach the locomotive. (Porter's tale of the West was actually filmed in New Jersey.)

building, ultimately saving the two imperiled victims from a fiery death.

There is some debate about the rescue sequence. Two versions exist. One shows the victims' perspective and then repeats the entire rescue from the firemen's point of view. The other version is even more sophisticated. It is "crosscut," which means that a little bit of each perspective is seen, back and forth, as the rescue unfolds. The debate centers on whether it was Porter who made the crosscut version or whether those edits were undertaken by someone else a few years later.

Porter's next film, *The Great Train Robbery*, uses scene shifts to portray changes in time. The movie, as you might imagine, tells the story of a train robbery from beginning to end. Robbers enter a telegraph office and tie up the telegraph officer to prevent him from warning the crew of a train. The bandits board the train, shoot a trainman, rob the passengers, and shoot a man who tries to resist. They proceed to the locomotive, jump off, reach their horses, and ride away into the shelter of the woods.

Porter then manipulates time through the use of editing. The action returns to the telegraph office. We see a sequence that is obviously taking place at the same time as the robbers are plundering the train. The telegraph operator is discovered, and tells lawmen what has happened. A posse sets out to catch the robbers, who meet their downfall in a climactic shoot-out.

The final scene is a close-up, showing only the head and arms of one of the robbers, who is facing the camera and firing straight at it. (When the movie was delivered to theaters, it was accompanied by a note saying that the gunshot scene could be shown as either the opening or the closing sequence.) *The Great Train Robbery* was an instant hit with audiences and is still dissected regularly by film scholars around the world.

D.W. Griffith's *Birth of a Nation* (1915)

Any serious discussion of D.W. Griffith's *Birth of a Nation* is invariably two-pronged, centering both on the technical merit of the movie and on its controversial story line.

Based on the Thomas Dixon novel *The Clansman*, *Birth of a Nation*, set during the period of reconstruction that followed the Civil War, is the story of two families, the Stonemans, who are from the North, and the Camerons, who are from the South.

The prevailing theme is a racist promotion of white supremacy that is conveyed by continuing attacks on the concept of miscegenation. Word of the controversial subject matter leaked out before the movie was released, causing protests across the country. Griffith was even accused of resurrecting the Ku Klux Klan, which had disbanded, but which reunited on Thanksgiving night, 1915, to celebrate the opening of his movie.

Griffith apparently never understood why people thought the movie was racist; he insisted that it was a true portrayal based on his own family's troubles adjusting to the war and its repercussions.

Birth of a Nation was photographed by Griffith's favorite cameraman, Billy Bitzer, using one camera. Bitzer used mirrors to reflect the sun when he needed light; he lay on the ground and let horses run over him to film the battle scenes. To create a special focus, Griffith and Bitzer blacked out the edges of a scene, enclosing it in a circle surrounded by black. Throughout the story, Griffith conveyed mood by returning to a particular street scene. The people, the lighting, and the activity there were used as a barometer to show the movie's mood at a particular moment.

Probably because of its controversial message, *Birth of a Nation* was an immediate commercial success and remains a favorite subject among students of film history, U.S. history, and the social sciences.

York, to Hollywood, California, to take advantage of the latter's "350 days of sunshine." Attractive real estate deals had already induced other producers to set up studios in Hollywood, where competition for patents, audiences, and actors had already created the entertainment phenomenon we still know today. The stars of the silent era, such as Mary Pickford (1893–1979), Dorothy (1898–1968) and Lillian Gish (1893–1993), Charlie Chaplin (1889–1977), Douglas Fairbanks (1883–1939), Greta Garbo (1905–1990), and Rudolph Valentino (1895–1926), completed the Hollywood pageant of the early 1900s. Griffith made movies throughout the decade, although none was as memorable as *Birth of a Nation*. His reign as top director was eventually eclipsed by a showman who specialized in great spectacles, Cecil Blount De Mille.

As the Roaring Twenties began, and as D.W. Griffith's pop-

Intolerance (1916)

In 1916 Griffith made *Intolerance*, in which he told four stories: three historical tales and the reworking of a modern story, "The Mother and the Law." The stories were set in different locations: Babylon in the sixth century B.C.; Jerusalem at the time of the persecution of Christ; Reformation France in the sixteenth century; and the slums of New York City in the twentieth century.

Griffith edited the film to tell the four stories simultaneously, tying them together with common devices. One device involved a woman, played by his favorite actress, Lillian Gish, peacefully rocking a cradle in a hazy white light, a portrayal inspired by Walt Whitman's *Leaves of Grass*. Audiences were anxious to see what Griffith would do after the enormous impact of *Birth of a Nation*, but word-of-mouth quickly spread that *Intolerance* was too complicated and convoluted to comprehend, and in a short time audience interest tapered off.

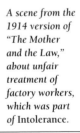

A scene from the 1914 version of "The Mother and the Law," about unfair treatment of factory workers, which was part of Intolerance.

Cecil B. De Mille (1881–1959)

In the early days of Hollywood, many of the actors and actresses who earned star status soon became troublesome to their studios, much as they do today. Many demanded more money, others developed personal problems brought on by the vagaries of instant stardom, and most were susceptible to the generous offers of competing studios. One director, Cecil B. De Mille, convinced his bosses that he could make successful movies without using stars.

Born in Ashfield, Massachusetts, in 1881, De Mille first went to Hollywood in 1913 as a playwright and actor, and was soon working for Adolph Zukor and Jesse Lasky at Paramount.

De Mille always had a taste for the lavish, which was evident both on the screen and in his personal tastes and behavior. He worked in an ornately decorated office and insisted that assistants trail him constantly, ready with a chair when he wanted to sit or an empty hand when he wanted to let go of something.

In his early movies De Mille tantalized a rather puritanical audience, first by dressing his actresses in outlandish costumes, then by setting scenes in bathrooms and bedrooms, where the camera had never gone before. Many early De Mille movies, such as *Why Change Your Wife?* and *The Golden Bed*, deliberately suggested moral ambiguity, although they always had honorable conclusions.

At first, De Mille's films featured extravagant sets and often included a grand event, such as a magnificent ball or splendid banquet. Eventually, he turned to subject matter that was grand in itself. He became the uncontested master of biblical and historical epics with such productions as *The Ten Commandments* (1923), *Ben-Hur* (1926), *King of Kings* (1927), *Cleopatra* (1934), and his greatest spectacle of all, the 1956 remake of *The Ten Commandments*.

Cecil B. DeMille poses for the camera to promote his 1935 Paramount release, The Crusades.

ularity began to wane, filmmaking came to be dominated more and more by De Mille and a man named King Vidor (1894–1982), whose gift for directing drama was first highlighted in *The Big Parade* (1925), and later in *The Crowd* (1928) and *The Fountainhead* (1949). By the middle of the twenties, however, theater attendance began to decline, and the studios clamored for new gimmicks to lure the public back.

The camera and camera operator were isolated in a soundproof booth so that the noise of the machinery would not be recorded.

Talkies

In an inspired effort to expand their small company, four brothers, Harry, Sam, Albert, and Jack Warner, decided to gamble on a machine called the Vitaphone, which would provide sound for their silent pictures. Developed by Bell Telephone technicians, the Vitaphone had been rejected by many other studios as too much of a novelty. But on August 6, 1926, the Warner brothers presented a Vitaphone musical score as accompaniment to a silent film called *Don Juan*. The presentation was preceded by an intro-ductory talk about the Vitaphone delivered by Will Hays, President of the Motion Picture Producers and Distributors of America. Audiences were receptive and demanded more movies with sound. The Warner brothers then produced the film that many historians consider the first talking picture, *The Jazz Singer*, starring Al Jolson (1886–1950), and released it in October 1927. It was in *The Jazz Singer* that Jolson spoke the famous, prophetic words "Wait a minute....You ain't heard nothin' yet."

Birth Pains of the Talkie

In the beginning, making pictures with sound was extremely awkward. First, there was the problem of the microphone. Because the single microphone was immobile, activity on the set was limited to the device's immediate area. Then there was the problem of hiding or disguising the microphone (parodied in *Singin' in the Rain*). Action was further restricted because the motion picture cameras were noisy and had to be isolated to mute their whirring sounds, thus rendering them immobile as well. Recording both picture and sound simultaneously took hours, and the machines created unbearable heat as time passed, ultimately requiring production to come to a halt so the equipment, and the actors, could cool off a little.

In his earliest Hollywood production, *Applause* (1929), a onetime New York City theater director named Rouben Mamoulian (1897–1987) is credited with solving the primary microphone dilemma

In the mid-1930s, Rouben Mamoulian was an innovator in the use of Technicolor.

by using two microphones simultaneously, then mixing the sound.

In some ways, *The Jazz Singer* can be called the first movie musical. The story of a cantor's son, played by Jolson, who wants to break family tradition and sing jazz for entertainment, the film contains a musical score and several songs sung by Jolson, including "Mammy" and "Blue Skies." *The Jazz Singer* was not technically perfect, but it revived the public's interest in movies and inspired a new burst of creativity in filmmakers.

"Talking pictures" transformed many movie careers. Such big stars of the silent screen as Pola Negri (1899–1987), Norma Talmadge (1897–1957), and John Gilbert (1897–1936) had voices that did not work well in "talkies." As a result, their careers soon fizzled. Others, most notably Greta Garbo, made a spectacular transition from the silent to the talking screen. The need for actors with strong and pleasing voices sent Hollywood producers eastward to Broadway, where they quickly signed stage performers to star in their films. As a result, many of the first talking pictures were simply remakes of successful stage productions.

Early musicals, such as *Hollywood Revue* (1929), and several versions of *Broadway Melody*, were advertised as "All talking! All singing! All dancing!" War stories, popular literature, slapstick comedy, and westerns all found their audiences as well. During the thirties, at the height of the Big Band era, studios made movies based on popular musicians and their bands. In 1939, technology, ambition, business savvy, and talent culminated in the making of a musical that has proven to be one of Hollywood's all-time classics, *The Wizard of Oz*.

The Wizard of Oz

Metro-Goldwyn-Mayer Studios was formed in 1924 when theater owner Marcus Loewe figured out that the best way to keep the lion's share of profits from the movies shown in his theaters would be to own the production companies, too. Consequently, he bought both the Metro Picture Company and the Goldwyn

Toto looks on as Dorothy sings "Over the Rainbow" somewhere in Kansas.

L. Frank Baum novel *The Wizard of Oz* and hired Mervyn LeRoy as executive producer of the movie. In fact, Mayer had just hired LeRoy away from Warner Brothers, where he had successfully produced or directed many movies, including *Little Caesar* and *Gold Diggers of 1933*. *The Wizard of Oz* was going to be different from other musicals; instead of being about singers and dancers, this would be a fairy tale about a little girl from Kansas who gets caught in a tornado and embarks on a fantastic adventure in an enchanting place, the land of Oz.

Picture Company, then brought in Louis B. Mayer, another theater owner, to run production. Under Mayer, MGM produced the *Broadway Melody* musicals in 1929, 1936, 1938, and 1940, and the Hardy Family episodic movies starring Lewis Stone, Fay Holden, and Mickey Rooney.

At a time when movie musicals all featured similar themes—either revamped versions of stage plays or backstage tales of romance and intrigue—MGM, under Mayer's direction, bought the rights to the

Production of the fantastic story required spectacular sets and costumes as well as brilliant music and casting. Many last-minute changes were made before production was completed. For example, a prince and princess were proposed as characters in the original story, but didn't make the final screenplay. W.C. Fields was offered the dual role of the professor-wizard, but he turned it down, and it was given to Frank Morgan (1890–1949), who was already under MGM contract. And, although there was much talk about "borrowing" Shirley Temple from Twentieth Century-Fox, producers decided to give the role of Dorothy Gale to a promising newcomer named Judy Garland.

In the original cast, Buddy Ebsen (b. 1908) and Ray Bolger (1904–1987), both popular song-and-dance men from the stage, were cast as the Scarecrow and the Tin Man, respectively. When the Cowardly Lion character was added to the story, producers immediately thought of another popular stage actor, Bert Lahr (1895–1967), for the role. But Ebsen hurt his leg during rehearsals and traded roles with Bolger. Ebsen then discovered that he was allergic to the metallic costuming paint of the Tin Man, and was ultimately replaced by another familiar actor, Jack Haley (1900–1979).

There were also several directorial changes, including a short stint by George Cukor (1899–1983), a Broadway director whose specialty was making movies out of theater productions, and who was preparing to direct Gone With The Wind (1939). Principal direction on The Wizard of Oz was completed by and credited to Victor Fleming (1883–1949), a cameraman-turned-director, who would follow Cukor to Gone With the Wind. King Vidor directed Oz's last few days, which included the sepia-toned Kansas scenes at the beginning and end of the movie.

The songs were written by the team of E.Y. Harburg (1896–1981) and Harold Arlen (1905–1946). "Over the Rainbow" won the Academy Award for Best Song of the year, and the musical score, which was under the musical direction of Herbert Stothart (1885–1949), won the Academy Award for Best Score (most of the other awards in 1939 went to Gone With the Wind). Ironically, the producers argued about whether or not to include the song "Over the Rainbow," and even previewed the movie for audiences both with and without the song. Associate producer Arthur Freed (1894–1973), who would go on to produce many of MGM's musicals, steadfastly argued in favor of keeping the song in the movie, and finally won the debate.

Easter Parade

Judy Garland went on to star in such movies as *Babes in Arms* (1939) and *Meet Me in St. Louis* (1944). In 1947, she was to be in a musical called *Easter Parade* with Gene Kelly and Ann Miller. This movie was a story about the breakup of a dance team, played by Kelly and Miller. The plot centered around a young dancer, played by Garland, who is brought in to be Kelly's new partner and soon falls in love with him.

During rehearsals, Gene Kelly broke his ankle, causing him to withdraw from the film rather than cause a costly delay of several weeks. The producers and Kelly recruited a movie and dancing star who was already in his second year of self-imposed retirement—Fred Astaire—and lured him into taking the role with the prospect of starring with Judy Garland and dancing to the score by Irving Berlin (1888–1989).

Fred Astaire and Judy Garland are "A Couple of Swells" in Easter Parade.

Garland and Astaire made a wonderful pair, especially in "A Couple of Swells." This movie contains many memorable

Judy Garland (1922–1969)

There may never be a movie star who rose more quickly or crashed more explosively than Judy Garland. Born Frances Gumm to vaudeville parents in 1922, Judy was a seasoned performer by the time she was five years old and a featured singer on popular radio programs by her early teens. Her first movie, *Broadway Melody 1938,* made her a star, and she immediately joined the production of *The Wizard of Oz,* hailed as a classic as soon as it premiered.

After Oz, Garland made a quick succession of movies, most of them for producer Arthur Freed, including *Babes in Arms* (1939), her first of many with Mickey Rooney. She then starred in *Strike Up The Band, Little Nellie Kelly, Babes on Broadway, For Me and My Gal,* and *Meet Me In St. Louis,* all by 1944.

During that prolific period of moviemaking, Judy began to take ill, more and more seriously and frequently. Many movie historians insist that the studios provided stimulating drugs to enhance performers' energy levels by day, then depressants to help them sleep at night. At any rate, it was during this period that Garland acquired what would become a lifelong dependency on drugs that contributed to her premature death in 1969.

Liza Minelli, Garland's daughter with director Vincente Minelli, has carried on her mother's craft, proving herself to be an equally scintillating talent. Judy Garland is still revered by countless fans who adore her waiflike portrayals, her beautiful, compelling voice, and her fortitude in the face of what must have been unrelenting personal unhappiness.

Hollywood's darling, Judy Garland.

Fred Astaire (1899–1987)

Fred Astaire and Ginger Rogers in Swing Time, *from which the song "The Way You Look Tonight" won an Oscar in 1936.*

When *Gay Divorcee* closed, Adele married and quit the partnership to live with her husband in England. An apprehensive Astaire starred alone in his first movie, *Flying Down To Rio* (1933), in which he was paired with a casual acquaintance named Ginger Rogers. That pairing proved highly successful. Together, Astaire and Rogers went on to star in *Top Hat, Swing Time, Shall We Dance,* and their final collaborative effort, *The Story of Vernon and Irene Castle* (1939).

By 1939, Rogers had decided to strike out on her own, and Astaire began to think about retirement, but that didn't last long. He starred with Eleanor Powell in *Broadway Melody 1940,* made some movies with Rita Hayworth, then teamed with another new partner, Bing Crosby, who was Astaire's costar in *Holiday Inn* and *Blue Skies.*

After starring with Judy Garland in *Easter Parade* (1948), Astaire made several more movies throughout the 1950s, including *Royal Wedding,* the film version of *The Band Wagon, Silk Stockings,* and *Funny Face.* Beginning in 1959, Astaire starred in three consecutive television specials, after which he continued to accept nondancing acting roles until his death in 1987.

Fred Astaire was born in Omaha, Nebraska, in 1899 and was dancing by the time he was five years old. He and his older sister Adele danced together throughout their childhood, achieved early recognition and success, and went to New York to perform on Broadway in *Over The Top* (1917). Fred began a lasting friendship with George Gershwin in New York, and the Astaire partners traveled between London and New York to perform in *The Band Wagon* (1931) and *Gay Divorcee* (1932).

Busby Berkeley (1895–1976)

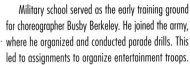

In the early 1930s, a choreographer-turned-director developed a characteristic movie musical style that in time came to be known simply by his name: Busby Berkeley.

Military school served as the early training ground for choreographer Busby Berkeley. He joined the army, where he organized and conducted parade drills. This led to assignments to organize entertainment troops. From the service, he entered the world of show business, and his first big break came when he was hired to choreograph the movie *42nd Street* (1933) for Warner Brothers.

42nd Street was received with great enthusiasm, and Berkeley went on to combine his military drill expertise with his dance talents to choreograph or direct *Babes in Arms, Strike Up The Band, Footlight Parade, Ziegfeld Girl, Lady Be Good,* and *Million Dollar Mermaid.* In his distinctive style, using a single camera to film musical numbers consisting of huge choruses in synchronized dance (sometimes performed underwater in a swimming pool), he frequently used elaborate props such as grand pianos, as in *Gold Diggers of 1935.*

Busby Berkeley is superimposed over a still from The Gold Diggers of 1933, *in which Joan Blondell sings "Remember the Forgotten Man," a tribute to the unemployed men who fought in World War I.*

Kathryn Grayson
(b. 1924)

Zelma Kathryn Elisabeth Hedrick changed her name to Kathryn Grayson and began her movie career before she was twenty, in *Andy Hardy's Private Secretary*. The dark-haired actress with the virtuous face and beautiful singing voice became one of MGM's favorite musical stars, and appeared in *Anchors Aweigh*; *Kiss Me, Kate* (also starring Howard Keel, her costar in *Show Boat*); *The Kissing Bandit*; *Till the Clouds Roll By*; *Thousands Cheer*; *Lovely to Look At*; *Two Sisters from Boston*; and the 1951 remake of *Show Boat*. She also starred in many other movies, including *So This is Love*, *Desert Song*, and *Vagabond King*.

musical numbers, including the title song, "I Love a Piano," "It Only Happens When I Dance with You," and "Steppin' Out with My Baby," in which Astaire, with brilliant technical assistance, performs an unforgettable slow-motion solo in front of a large chorus of dancers performing at full speed.

Show Boat

Show Boat, a book written by Edna Ferber, was originally adapted for the Broadway stage by Oscar Hammerstein II (1895–1960) and Jerome Kern (1885–1945) in 1927 with great success. Hammerstein filmed *Show Boat* in 1936, starring Irene Dunne (1904–1990), Allan Jones (1907–1992), Helen Morgan (1900–1941), and Paul Robeson (1898–1976). Because of the continuing relevance of the story and the beauty of the musical score, producer Arthur Freed decided to remake the film in 1951, starring Kathryn Grayson, Howard Keel, Ava Gardner (1922–1990), and William Warfield (b. 1920).

Set on a Mississippi riverboat, *Show Boat* follows the lives of several people

living on and around the river at the turn of the century and portrays their struggles to survive in the racially charged atmosphere of the South. *Show Boat* contains several unforgettable songs, including William Warfield's ardent rendition of "Ol' Man River," "Can't Help Lovin' That Man," and the inspirational "Make Believe," sung by lovers Magnolia (Kathryn Grayson) and Gaylord (Howard Keel).

Singin' in the Rain

In 1952, MGM produced *Singin' in the Rain*, a classic often considered to be Hollywood's preeminent musical. Starring Gene Kelly, Donald O'Connor (b. 1925), Debbie Reynolds (b. 1932), Millard Mitchell (1900–1953), and Jean Hagen

Gene Kelly, "Singin' in the Rain," in what is perhaps the archetypal scene from a Hollywood musical.

Howard Keel (b. 1917)

Howard Keel's first movie role was in a 1948 British film entitled *The Small Voice*. Thanks to his singing talents and rugged good looks, he soon became one of the most popular and enduring actors through the fifties and sixties, starring in such musicals as *Annie Get Your Gun, Calamity Jane, Seven Brides for Seven Brothers*, and *Kismet*. He also starred in westerns, including *Waco, The War Wagon*, and *Red Tomahawk*. Millions of television viewers throughout the 1980s knew Howard Keel as good-guy Clayton Farrow on the long-lasting prime-time soap opera *Dallas*.

Howard Keel, the quintessential masculine screen persona.

(1923–1977), the story is a spoof about Hollywood's shift from the silent movie to the talkie.

In *Singin' in the Rain*, a famous silent-screen star with a horrendous voice and a tremendous ego, played by Jean Hagen, is cast to star in a film that becomes a talkie, then a musical, despite her numerous limitations. The producers decide to use a starlet, played by Debbie Reynolds, as her vocal stand-in—without the star's knowledge, of course. This clever, sometimes cynical, often hilarious movie features fantastic dancing, slapstick comedy, and many memorable musical numbers, including "Good Mornin'," "Fit as a Fiddle," and "Make 'em Laugh," in which Donald O'Connor literally dances on the walls.

The lyrical "Broadway Ballet" sequence, featuring Gene Kelly and Cyd Charisse (b. 1923), was choreographed by Kelly himself, as was the most memorable number in the movie, during which Kelly playfully splashes up and down a street curb in a steady downpour, with only a black umbrella and a lamppost for props.

Gene Kelly (1912–1996)

Most movie historians agree that Hollywood nurtured into stardom two great male dancers: Fred Astaire and Gene Kelly. Broadway and movie musicals were at the height of their popularity when Gene Kelly made his movie debut for producer Arthur Freed in *For Me and My Gal* (1942), also starring Judy Garland.

Gene Kelly began his career as a choreographer in New York, then was discovered by dance director Robert Alton (1906–1957) and signed to star on the Broadway stage in *Pal Joey* (1940). After moving to Hollywood to star in *For Me and My Gal,* Kelly continued to star in a string of Hollywood musicals, including *DuBarry Was a Lady, Cover Girl, Anchors Aweigh* (in which Kelly performed with cartoon characters Tom and Jerry), *Ziegfeld Follies, The Pirate* (again costarring Judy Garland), *On Your Toes,* and the 1951 musical that received the Best Picture Oscar, the stunning *An American In Paris.*

After *Singin' in the Rain,* which was an enormous success, and *Brigadoon,* audience interest in musicals began to wane. Kelly expanded the range of his acting talents to include drama, starring in *Marjorie Morningstar,* with Natalie Wood, and *Inherit the Wind* (1960). He also directed several movies, including the film version of *Hello, Dolly!* (1969) and *The Cheyenne Social Club* (1970).

Brigadoon

Alan Jay Lerner (1918–1986) wrote *Brigadoon* for the Broadway stage in 1947, and MGM decided to produce the movie in 1954, starring Gene Kelly, who had been waiting for the right role since his triumphant performance two years earlier in *Singin' in the Rain*.

This story is a fairy tale about two New York bachelors, played by Kelly and a very funny Van Johnson (b. 1916), who stumble into a town in Scotland named Brigadoon that awakens for only one day every one hundred years. In Brigadoon, Kelly's character falls in love with Fiona, played by Cyd Charisse. Kelly requested Charisse to play the role because he had admired her performance in *Singin' in the Rain*.

Kelly's instincts were correct, for their dance to "The Heather on the Hill" is a beautiful and romantic ballet. The dancing and the songs, particularly "Almost Like Being in Love" and "From This Day On," together with the exquisite, though not totally realistic, sets that were forced on director Vincente Minelli (1913–1986)

Above: Gene Kelly and Cyd Charisse dance to "Heather on the Hill." Opposite: Gordon MacRae sings "Surrey with the Fringe on Top" to Shirley Jones in Oklahoma!

because increasing production costs prohibited filming in Scotland or even on location in California, make the movie a thoroughly enjoyable fantasy.

Oklahoma!

One of the more successful Broadway plays to make it to the big screen was *Oklahoma!*, produced on stage in 1943 by Richard Rodgers (1902–1979) and Oscar Hammerstein II after Hammerstein rewrote the Lynn Riggs play *Green Grow the Lilacs*. The same team produced the musical for film

Gordon MacRae
(1921–1986)

With his handsome face, all-American demeanor, and strong baritone voice, Gordon MacRae was a natural for the strong lead roles in *Oklahoma!* and *Carousel*. First noticed in an unremarkable film entitled *The Big Punch* (1948), MacRae was cast in many more movies for Warner Brothers, beginning in 1949 with *Look for the Silver Lining*, starring June Haver (b. 1925). His career included roles in *Tea For Two*, *The West Point Story*, and *By the Light of the Silvery Moon*—all costarring Doris Day (b. 1924)—and *The Daughter of Rosie O'Grady*, *Three Girls and a Sailor*, *The Desert Song* (costarring Kathryn Grayson), and *The Best Things in Life Are Free* (1956).

in 1955, starring Gordon MacRae, Shirley Jones, and Rod Steiger (b. 1925).

Set in the territory of Oklahoma during the period when it verged on statehood, *Oklahoma!* is a love story about two men—one wholesome, one gruff—vying for the same woman. The Rodgers and Hammerstein score, which included ensemble dance numbers and the songs "Oh, What a Beautiful Morning" and "Surrey with the Fringe on Top," won the Academy Award for 1955. *Oklahoma!* is exemplary of the Rodgers and Hammerstein style, which made the musical score a useful storytelling tool instead of a musical interruption in the story.

The King and I

A true story based on the autobiography by Anna Leonowens—particularly the part about her life as a governess in the court of Siam—was adapted several times before it finally evolved into the 1956 movie musical *The King and I*.

Leonowens' story was rewritten by Margaret Landon and entitled *Anna and*

Yul Brynner and Deborah Kerr dance in the monarch's palace.

The King of Siam, then made into a 1946 movie starring Rex Harrison and Irene Dunne. In 1951 the story was produced as an extravagant musical play on Broadway by Rodgers and Hammerstein, starring Yul Brynner and Gertrude Lawrence (1900–1952). When it was decided to make the movie, Deborah Kerr (b. 1921) was given the part of Anna, and Brynner was chosen to re-create the role of the king, which won him the Academy Award that year, and for which he will always be remembered. The movie contained several outstanding musical numbers, including "Hello, Young Lovers" and "Getting to Know You," as well as "Shall We Dance?"

Carousel

Rodgers and Hammerstein brought *Carousel* to Broadway in 1945, then made the movie version in 1956. Using a popular fantasy theme, the juxtaposition of life and afterlife, *Carousel* is about a carnival barker who is killed during a burglary and now "looks down" at the woman he loved

Yul Brynner (1920–1985)

Yul Brynner had a career that included many brilliant performances, yet he will always be remembered best as the King of Siam in *The King and I*. Not only was he suited to the role, but he loved it, and continued to portray the King of Siam virtually until his death.

Brynner's first movie role was in *Port of New York* (1949). Two years later, he shaved his head for the role of the monarch in *The King and I*, bringing him acclaim for his acting presence and attention for his sexy bald look, which he retained throughout his career.

Onstage, his large stature and deep, strong voice commanded attention. His other outstanding performances included roles in the 1956 version of *The Ten Commandments*, *Anastasia*, *The Brothers Karamazov*, *The Sound and the Fury*, *Solomon and Sheba*, *The*

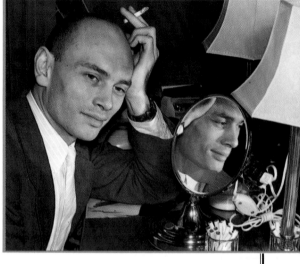

Yul Brynner backstage in 1951, in between Broadway performances of The King and I.

Magnificent Seven, *Once More With Feeling*, *Westworld*, and *Futureworld*.

and the daughter he never knew. Gordon MacRae and Shirley Jones play the lovers whose romance never runs smoothly, and their song, "If I Loved You," is interwoven throughout the entire story as an emotional thread that ties the broken family together. The song "You'll Never Walk Alone" expresses a recurring theme of faith and courage that also winds through the story, culminating when MacRae returns from heaven to visit his daughter on her graduation day. Filled with lyrical music, dancing, and romance, *Carousel* remains impressive entertainment today.

South Pacific

Wartime romance is the theme of another Rodgers and Hammerstein musical, *South Pacific*, produced for the stage in 1949 and for the screen in 1956 with Mitzi Gaynor as devoted navy nurse Nellie Forbush,

and Rossano Brazzi (b. 1916) as Emile de Becque, a mysterious French man who is first suspected of being a spy, but turns out to be a hero.

Above: Rosanno Brazzi romances Mitzi Gaynor. Left: Gordon MacRae and Shirley Jones as the ill-fated lovers in Carousel.

Cultural influences and frustrated romance inspire imaginative music in *South Pacific*, such as Gaynor's "I'm Gonna Wash That Man Right Outta My Hair," and "Younger Than Springtime," "Happy Talk," and "Bali Ha'i." The combination of an enduring love story, set against a wartime backdrop, with lavish locations and scenery and an unforgettable score makes *South Pacific* a classic work that is regularly produced onstage even today.

Gigi

Movie producer Arthur Freed became interested in the 1948 French film *Gigi*, based on a book by Colette, at about the

Francesca Mitzi de Czanyi von Gerber, better known as Mitzi Gaynor, began her career in 1950 at the age of nineteen. A skilled dancer with an engaging singing voice, Miss Gaynor soon came to star in many Hollywood musicals, including *My Blue Heaven*, *Golden Girl*, *Bloodhounds of Broadway*, *There's No Business Like Show Business*, *Surprise Package* (also starring Yul Brynner), *Anything Goes*, *The Joker Is Wild*, *Les Girls*, and, of course, *South Pacific*. In the 1970s and 1980s, she enjoyed singing engagements in special clubs and starred in several television specials.

same time that Broadway producers were also considering it for the stage. Freed acquired the rights first, however, and put together a movie production that was elaborate enough for Broadway.

The musical was an all-star affair. Alan Jay Lerner wrote the story and lyrics, Frederick Loewe (1901–1988) wrote the music, and André Previn (b. 1929) was music director. Vincente Minelli directed the movie and theater designer Cecil Beaton (1904–1980) was brought in to design the costumes and sets, many of which were replications of sites in Paris. (The legendary restaurant Maxim's actually closed for a week to accommodate the production.) Finally, in order to promote the lavish production, MGM premiered *Gigi* in a Broadway theater in 1958.

Freed's first task was to turn the original story, about a girl being raised, as both her mother and grandmother had been, to become a mistress for a wealthy man, into a story that would be deemed morally acceptable by Hollywood standards. Thus, the story became one in which Gigi, played by Leslie Caron (b. 1931), who is groomed to be a sophisticated and mature young woman, falls in love with the character played by Louis Jourdan (b. 1920). The cast also included Maurice Chevalier, coerced back from semiretirement by the lavish production, and Hermione Gingold, as friends who were once lovers. Their rendition of "I Remember It Well" is one of the highlights of the movie, because the actors, also friends, sang it with a natural tenderness not often seen in the movies.

All of the collaborators were rewarded on Academy Award night, when *Gigi* was named Best Picture: Vincente Minelli was

Maurice Chevalier (1888–1972)

With an acting career that spanned five decades, suave Frenchman Maurice Chevalier was one of Hollywood's favorite sophisticates. His first movie also happened to be Paramount's first musical, entitled *Innocents of Paris* (1929), in which he sang "Louise," the song that became his lifelong trademark. Immediately after, he starred in *The Love Parade* and *The Big Pond*, earning one Academy Award nomination in 1929 and another in 1930, then *The Smiling Lieutenant*, *The Merry Widow*, and an excellent musical comedy called *Love Me Tonight*.

Chevalier retired for several years before returning to the screen with roles in *Love in the Afternoon* (1957), *Can-Can* (1960), and the performance for which he is best remembered, his star turn in *Gigi*. Chevalier's last movie was *Monkeys Go Home*, made for Disney in 1966, when he was in his late seventies.

Maurice Chevalier poses in front of hundreds of boaters; his character in Gigi *wore one just like them.*

Hermione Gingold (1897–1987)

Hermione Gingold will always be best known for her performance opposite Maurice Chevalier in *Gigi*, yet she has quite a treasury of distinctive performances to her credit.

Often a bit eccentric and always unique, Gingold began her career in such British films as *Merry Comes To Town* (1937), *Meet Mr. Penny* (1938), and *The Pickwick Papers* (1952). She began making movies in the United States in the 1950s, and appeared in *Around the World in Eighty Days*; *Bell, Book and Candle*; *The Naked Edge*; *I'd Rather Be Rich*; *Promise Her Anything*; *The Music Man*; and *A Little Night Music*, in which she played the mother of Elizabeth Taylor's character. Her last role was in *Garbo Talks* (1984), with Anne Bancroft. She died three years later.

named Best Director; Alan Jay Lerner was named Best Writer; Lerner and Loewe were awarded Best Song ("Gigi"); André Previn received the award for Music Direction; and Cecil Beaton received an award for his costumes. Maurice Chevalier, who won the Golden Globe Award for his role in *Gigi*, was presented with an Honorary Special Award.

West Side Story

In 1961, United Artists filmed the successful Arthur Laurents play *West Side Story*, a modern version of Shakespeare's *Romeo and Juliet*. Laurents set the story on New York City streets, and transformed the Montagues and Capulets into two warring gangs, the Jets and the Sharks. The musical drama, with music by Leonard Bernstein (1918–1990), lyrics by Stephen Sondheim (b. 1930), and choreography by Jerome Robbins (b. 1918), still sparks emotion.

Inspired by earlier Rodgers and Hammerstein musical productions, Bernstein and Sondheim incorporated

Natalie Wood (1938–1981)

Natalie Wood had a life as compelling and dramatic as any Hollywood screenplay. She is remembered for performances that spanned a thirty-eight-year career marked with multiple marriages (two of them to actor Robert Wagner). Her career was tragically shortened by her accidental death at the age of forty-three.

Every year, audiences see her as a child in the Christmas favorite *Miracle on 34th Street* (1947). Later, as a teen, she starred in the classic *Rebel Without A Cause* (1955); as a young woman, she created several memorable roles, in *The Searchers* (1956), *All the Fine Young Cannibals*, *Splendor in the Grass*, *Marjorie Morningstar*, *West Side Story*, and *Love With the Proper Stranger*.

Her adult performances include roles in *This Property is Condemned*, *Bob & Carol & Ted & Alice*, and *Brainstorm*, which was in production at the time of her death.

music and dance into *West Side Story* to advance the story with lyric drama and electric tension. Virtually every scene is choreographed, almost like a ballet, making the few nonmusical scenes, usually those with dialogue, the exceptions in the storytelling.

Tony and Maria, the transposed Romeo and Juliet, declare their love in the song "Tonight," which is reprised later to highlight mounting anticipation of the conflict between central characters in the oppos-

Richard Beymer and Natalie Wood pledge their love on a fire escape in West Side Story.

ing gangs. The movie, starring Natalie Wood, Richard Beymer (b. 1939), Rita Moreno (b. 1931), George Chakiris (b. 1934), and Russ Tamblyn (b. 1935) won many Academy Awards, including Best Picture, Best Director (Robert Wise [b. 1914] and Jerome Robbins as codirectors), Best Supporting Actress (Moreno), and Best Supporting Actor (Chakiris).

The Music Man

The Music Man is probably the quintessential all-American musical. Produced first on Broadway in 1957, from a Meredith Willson (1902–1984) book, Warner studios hired director Morton daCosta (1914–1989) to bring it to the screen in 1962.

In the movie version of *The Music Man*, Robert Preston plays a con man who comes to River City, Iowa, ostensibly to build a boys' band, but really to swindle the townspeople out of band funds. He meets Marion Paroo (Shirley Jones), who falls for him, and a little boy played by Ron Howard. All eventually turns out

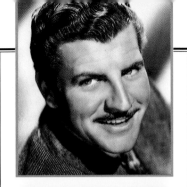

Robert Preston (1918–1987)

After his first few years in the movies, Robert Preston was constantly switching his allegiance back and forth between the Broadway stage and films. After an early start, Preston gained notoriety in Cecil B. De Mille's *Union Pacific* (1939) opposite Barbara Stanwyck (1907–1990), then made many more movies, including *Typhoon, Beau Geste, Reap the Wild Wind, This Gun For Hire,* and *The Macomber Affair.* He spent much of the 1950s on Broadway, playing in such shows as *The Lion In Winter* and *Twentieth Century,* and he won the Tony Award for both *The Music Man* (in a role he would re-create in the film) and *I Do! I Do!*

Preston played the father in *The Dark At The Top of The Stairs* (1960), and starred in *All the Way Home, Child's Play, Mame, Semi-Tough, Victor/Victoria,* and *The Last Starfighter* (1984).

Voice-overs

Singin' in the Rain is a hilarious portrayal of the real-life struggles of Hollywood stars making the transition from silent to talking movies. Jean Hagen's character has a voice so screechy and painful to the ear that the producers conspire to hide Debbie Reynolds behind the scenes to "be her voice." The movie is fiction, of course, but the situation is based on reality.

An early example of this situation was the 1951 version of *Show Boat*. Producers agreed that Ava Gardner was perfect for the role of Julie, and she was. The only problem was that she wasn't an experienced singer. Gardner made a great effort, however, and did sing the songs written for Julie, but nervous producers were skeptical, so they tested several women to find the voice that most closely matched Gardner's, then hired Annette Warren to record all of Julie's songs. When the movie was completed, the studio previewed it with both vocal tracks before finally deciding to release the movie with Warren's singing voice. They then rerecorded the soundtrack album, releasing it with Gardner's voice.

Marni Nixon's voice was heard around the world, but her face was not at all familiar to the moviegoing public.

Besides Annette Warren, popular voice doubles included Marni Nixon, Anita Ellis, and Carole Richards, all of whom enjoyed successful careers. Marni Nixon sang Deborah Kerr's songs in *The King and I* and Natalie Wood's songs in *West Side Story*. It wasn't only women who needed vocal doubles; Jim Bryant sang for Richard Beymer in *West Side Story*.

well, as exemplified in the song "Till There Was You," sung first by Shirley Jones and reprised near the end by Preston. "Seventy-Six Trombones," in which Preston leads the town in a vigor- ous musical extravaganza, underscores the movie's enthusiasm and spirit.

Musical director Ray Heindorf (1908–1980) received an Academy Award for his work in *The Music Man*, which runs two hours and thirty-one minutes. Audiences didn't seem to mind the length; they made it the year's top-grossing film.

My Fair Lady

My Fair Lady, the Broadway musical version of the George Bernard Shaw play *Pygmalion,* was written by Lerner and Loewe and starred Rex Harrison (1908–1990) and Julie Andrews. When Jack Warner decided to produce the film version of the play, he insisted on using current box-office star Audrey Hepburn instead of Julie Andrews in the role of Eliza Dolittle.

My Fair Lady is the story of a flower-selling cockney street girl who falls under the tutelage of the elitist Henry Higgins, played by Harrison, who accepts a challenge to turn her into a "duchess." The

Right: *The servants help Eliza Doolittle (Audrey Hepburn) get ready for bed.* **Below:** Robert Preston leads the River City band in **The Music Man.**

Audrey Hepburn (1929–1993)

Audrey Hepburn had a presence that made her a star the first time she appeared onscreen; she won the 1953 Academy Award for Best Actress for her screen debut as a princess traveling incognito in *Roman Holiday*. From there she continued to turn out memorable performances in many movies, including *Sabrina*, *Breakfast at Tiffany's*, *Funny Face*, *Love in the Afternoon*, *Green Mansions*, *Charade*, *Wait Until Dark* (in which she played a blind woman targeted by drug pushers), *My Fair Lady*, *Two for the Road*, and *Robin and Marian*. In the 1980s, Hepburn's role as ambassador for UNICEF took precedence over her interest in acting, and she devoted her time and energy to that organization's efforts until her death early in 1993. Hepburn was posthumously honored at the 1993 Academy Awards with the Jean Jersholt Humanitarian Award.

movie, like the play, is filled with clever and memorable songs, such as "With a Little Bit O' Luck," "On the Street Where You Live," "Get Me to the Church on Time," and "I've Grown Accustomed to Her Face," as well as Eliza's "I Could Have Danced All Night," which she sings as she realizes she is beginning to fall in love with the professor.

Just as they had for the production of *Gigi*, Warner Brothers brought Cecil Beaton to the production to design the Academy Award–winning costumes. In 1964, *My Fair Lady* won an Oscar for Best

Picture, George Cukor received the Best Director Oscar, and Rex Harrison received the award for Best Actor. Noticeable among Oscar omissions that year was the nomination of Audrey Hepburn as Best Actress. Julie Andrews, who had accepted the role of Mary Poppins after being spurned by Jack Warner for the Eliza Doolittle part, won the Best Actress Oscar. Many critics speculated that Audrey Hepburn had not been nominated because she was not a singer; her songs in *My Fair Lady* were all performed by Marni Nixon (b. 1929).

The Sound of Music

After her success as Mary Poppins, Julie Andrews was in demand to play the role she had created onstage in *The Sound of Music*, a story based on the true story of the von Trapp family, in the movie version directed by Robert Wise.

Set in the breathtaking Austrian Alps just prior to World War II, the movie stars Andrews as the governess Maria and Christopher Plummer (b. 1929) as the

Maria (Julie Andrews) endears herself to the von Trapp children with a song in The Sound of Music. *The movie was such an overwhelming success that industry insiders dubbed it "The Sound of Money."*

widowed navy commander Baron von Trapp. Maria brings happiness back to the seven motherless von Trapp children, marries the Baron, and finally uses her love of music to help the family escape the Nazis, who are demanding that von

Julie Andrews took the role of Mary Poppins because Jack Warner did not hire her to star in the role of Eliza Doolittle in *My Fair Lady,* a role she had created on Broadway. Warner may have regretted that decision when Andrews won that year's Best Actress Oscar for her starring role in the Poppins fantasy. Subsequent roles in *The Sound of Music* and *Thoroughly Modern Millie* defined Julie Andrews as a pristine, virginal character until her husband, producer Blake Edwards, directed her in a series of sophisticated roles, beginning with *Darling Lili* (1970), and including *10* (1979), *S.O.B.* (1981), and *That's Life* (1986).

Julie Andrews and Dick van Dyke with cartoon turtles in **Mary Poppins.**

Trapp join their army. The Rodgers and Hammerstein songs, including "The Sound of Music," "Climb Every Mountain," sung by Peggy Wood (1892–1978), and Christopher Plummer's rendition of the patriotic "Edelweiss," are unsurpassed.

Irwin Kostal (b. 1915) received an Academy Award for musical direction,

Robert Wise received the Oscar for direction, and *The Sound of Music* was named Best Picture of 1965. Discerning ears can detect Marni Nixon, the prolific voice-double, in the role of Sister Sophia, especially in the song "How Do You Solve a Problem Like Maria?" sung by a convent ensemble.

Oliver!

By the late 1960s, the British decided to try their hand at movie musicals, and chose the Lionel Bart (b. 1930) play *Oliver!*, based on the Charles Dickens novel *Oliver Twist*. The screenplay was written by Vernon Harris (b. 1910) and the music by Lionel Bart, and Sir Carol Reed (1906–1976) was hired to direct his first musical. Columbia Pictures showed great courage when they decided to use a cast of British actors virtually unknown in America to play the vivid Dickens roles. *Oliver!* was completed in December 1968, and starred Ron Moody (b. 1924), Oliver Reed (b. 1938), Harry Secombe (b. 1921), and Mark Lester as Oliver.

The Dickens story, about a runaway orphan who becomes entangled with villains and lowlifes, proved to be both a critical and commercial success; at the Academy Awards it won the Oscar for Best

Picture. Carol Reed won Best Director and John Green (1908–1989) was awarded for Best Musical Direction of the Lionel Bart score, which included "As Long As He Needs Me," sung by Shani Wallis (b. 1933), "You've Got to Pick a Pocket or Two," and the poignant, melancholy "Where Is Love," sung by ten-year-old Mark Lester.

The End of an Era

The Hollywood musicals of the forties, fifties, and sixties will probably never be surpassed. Throughout the 1950s, most of the major studios budgeted for the production of two or three musicals a year, but by 1960, this was no longer so. Stars such as Fred Astaire, Gene Kelly, Shirley Jones, Julie Andrews, Yul Brynner, and Robert Preston focused on finding straight dramatic roles, and no one nurtured or encouraged the succeeding generation. The talent was there on the Broadway stage (Hal Prince [b. 1928], Bob Fosse [1927–1987], and Michael Bennett [1943–1987] to name just a few), but the interest in Hollywood was not. The costs were too great. Salaries, technical equipment, and post-production, advertising, and distribution costs had all skyrocketed, forcing new priorities at the studios. Gradually, the producers and directors who had been hailed for their great screen spectacles were nudged aside by

Oliver tries to hide, but is nabbed.

Hollywood's newest heroes, the "little producers" who could make hit movies for comparatively small amounts of money.

Audiences also became more sophisticated—some would say more cynical—during the sixties and seventies. Political events such as the Vietnam War and Watergate forced the eyes of a nation to open wide. Poverty, social unrest, and criminal violence escalated in the cities. The blight of drugs and crime spread—even to rural areas. The nation's divorce rate exploded. A roller-coaster economy brought frightening uncertainty to a generation raised to believe in the American Dream. Not surprisingly, Hollywood found it more and more difficult to amuse its audiences with tuneful tales of romantic love, no matter how extravagant the production.

Not that the Hollywood musical is dead. In recent decades, movies such as *Hair*, *Flashdance*, *La Bamba*, *A Chorus Line*, *For the Boys*, and *Newsies* tried to mine a particular lode of sentiment, but none succeeded in the same way or to nearly the same degree as had musicals from the

A scene from the movie version (1985) of one of the most popular Broadway musicals of all time, A Chorus Line.

previous age. And that's what it was—an age, an era that has passed and is unlikely to be resurrected except in memory.

Fortunately, the great movie musicals are preserved forever on videotape. Small audiences, which collectively amount to a large audience, will always be able to thrill to that extraordinary music generations later. These future audiences will continue to marvel at choreography that is unlikely to be surpassed, and will, perhaps, respond affectionately to a tuneful tale of romantic love that could only have been produced in Hollywood.

Bibliography

Applebaum, Stanley. *The Hollywood Musical: A Picture Quiz Book.* New York: Dover Publishing, 1974.

Blum, Daniel. *A Pictorial History of the Silent Screen.* New York: Putnam, 1953.

Boller, Paul F., Jr. *Hollywood Anecdotes.* New York: William Morrow & Co., 1987.

Brownlow, Kevin. *Hollywood: The Pioneers.* New York: Alfred A. Knopf, 1979.

Cohen, Daniel and Susan. *500 Great Films.* New York: Exeter Books, 1987.

Fordin, Hugh. *The World of Entertainment.* New York: Doubleday, 1975.

Griffith, Richard. *The Movie Stars.* New York: Doubleday, 1970.

Griffith, Richard, Eileen Bowser, and Arthur Mayer. *The Movies.* New York: Simon & Schuster, 1981.

Halliwell, Leslie. *Halliwell's Film Guide.* New York: Charles Scribner's Sons, 1991.

Hart, James, ed. *The Man Who Invented Hollywood: The Autobiography of D.W. Griffith.* Louisville, Ky.: Touchstone Publishing Company, 1972.

Kislan, Richard. *The Musical: A Look at the American Musical Theater.* Engle-wood Cliffs, N.J.: Prentice Hall, 1980.

Mast, Gerald, rev. by Bruce F. Kawin. *A Short History of the Movies.* New York: MacMillan, 1992.

Mordden, Ethan. *The Hollywood Studios: House Style in the Garden Age of Movies.* New York: Alfred A. Knopf, 1988.

Norman, Barry. *The Story of Hollywood.* New York: New American Library, 1987.

Peary, Danny. *Close-Ups.* New York: Workman Publishing, 1988.

Thomas, Tony. *That's Dancing!* New York: Harry N. Abrams, Inc., 1984.

Wiley, Mason, and Damien Bona. *Inside Oscar.* New York: Ballantine Books, 1988.

Further Reading

Barnes, Ken. *The Crosby Years.* New York: St. Martin's Press, 1980.

Freedland, Michael. *The Warner Brother.* New York: St. Martin's Press, 1983.

Giannetti, Louis, and Scott Eyman. *Flashback: A Brief History of Film.* Englewood Cliffs, N.J.: Prentice Hall, 1991.

Higham, Charles. *Merchant of Dreams: Louis B. Mayer, M.G.M., and the Secret of Hollywood.* New York: Donald I. Fine, Inc., 1993.

Hirschhorn, Clive. *The Hollywood Musical.* New York: Crown Publishing Company, 1981.

Jablonski, Edward. *Gershwin: A Biography.* New York: Doubleday, 1987.

Jewell, Richard B., with Vernon Harbin. *The RKO Story.* London: Arlington House, published by Octopus Books Limited, 1982.

Schatz, Thomas. *The Genius of the System: Hollywood Filmmaking in the Studio Era.* New York: Pantheon Books, 1988.

Thomas, Bob. *Clown Prince of Hollywood: The Antic Life and Times of Jack L. Warner.* New York: McGraw-Hill Publishing Company, 1990.

Recording Information

"Over The Rainbow"
Sung by Judy Garland, written by E.Y. Harburg and Harold Arlen
From *The Wizard of Oz,* produced in 1939 by Mervyn LeRoy for MGM
Written by Noel Langley, Florence Ryerson, and Edgar Allan Wolfe
Based on the novel by L. Frank Baum
Directed by Victor Fleming
Musical direction by Herbert Stothart

"A Couple of Swells"
Sung by Judy Garland and Fred Astaire, written by Irving Berlin
From *Easter Parade,* produced in 1948 by Arthur Freed for MGM
Written by Sidney Sheldon, Frances Goodrich, and Albert Hackett
Directed by Charles Walters
Musical direction by Roger Edens and Johnny Green

"Make Believe"
Sung by Kathryn Grayson and Howard Keel, written by Jerome Kern and Oscar Hammerstein II
From *Show Boat,* produced in 1951 by Arthur Freed for MGM
Written by John Lee Mahin from the play by Oscar Hammerstein II
Based on the book by Edna Ferber
Directed by George Sidney
Musical direction by Conrad Salinger and Adolph Deutsch

"Singin' in the Rain"
Sung by Gene Kelly, written by Nacio Herb Brown, with lyrics by Arthur Freed
From *Singin' in the Rain,* produced in 1952 by Arthur Freed for MGM
Written by Adolph Green and Betty Comden
Directed and choreographed by Gene Kelly and Stanley Donen
Musical direction by Lennie Hayton

"Almost Like Being in Love"
Sung by Gene Kelly, written by Frederick Loewe and Alan Jay Lerner
From *Brigadoon,* produced in 1954 by Arthur Freed for MGM
Written by Alan Jay Lerner from his play
Directed by Vincente Minelli
Musical direction by Johnny Green

"The Surrey With The Fringe On Top"
Sung by Gordon MacRae, written by Richard Rodgers and Oscar Hammerstein II

From *Oklahoma!,* produced in 1955 by Richard Rodgers, Oscar Hammerstein II, and Arthur Hornblow Jr. for Magna

Written by Oscar Hammerstein II, Sonya Levien, and William Ludwig

Based on the original play *Green Grow the Rushes,* by Lynn Riggs

Directed by Fred Zinnemann

Musical direction by Robert Russell Bennett, Jay Blackton, and Adolph Deutsch

"Shall We Dance?"

Sung by Yul Brynner and Marni Nixon, written by Richard Rodgers and Oscar Hammerstein II

From *The King and I,* produced in 1956 by Charles Brackett for TCF

Written by Ernest Lehman

Directed by Walter Lang

Musical direction by Alfred Newman and Ken Darby

"If I Loved You"

Sung by Shirley Jones and Gordon MacRae, written by Richard Rodgers and Oscar Hammerstein II

From *Carousel,* produced in 1956 by Henry Ephron for TCF

Written by Phoebe and Henry Ephron

Based on the play *Liliom,* by Forenc Molnar

Directed by Henry King

"I'm Gonna Wash That Man Right Outta My Hair"

Sung by Mitzi Gaynor, written by Richard Rodgers and Oscar Hammerstein II

From *South Pacific,* produced in 1958 by Buddy Adler and S.P. Enterprises for Magna

Written by Paul Osborn, Richard Rodgers, Oscar Hammerstein II, and Joshua Logan

Based on the novel *Tales of the South Pacific,* by James Michener

Directed by Joshua Logan

Musical direction by Alfred Newman and Ken Darby

"I Remember It Well"

Sung by Hermione Gingold and Maurice Chevalier, written by Alan Jay Lerner and Frederick Loewe

From *Gigi,* produced in 1958 by Arthur Freed for MGM

Written by Alan Jay Lerner

From the book *Gigi,* by Colette

Directed by Vincente Minelli

Musical direction by André Previn

"Tonight"

Sung by Marni Nixon and Jim Bryant, written by Leonard Bernstein and Stephen Sondheim

From *West Side Story,* produced in 1961 by Robert Wise for United Artists

Written by Ernest Lehman from the play by Arthur Laurents

Directed by Robert Wise and Jerome Robbins

"Seventy-Six Trombones"

Sung by Robert Preston and ensemble, written by Meredith Willson

From *The Music Man,* produced in 1962 by Morton da Costa for Warner

Written by Marion Hargrove from the play by Meredith Willson

Directed by Morton da Costa

Musical direction by Ray Heindorf

"I Could Have Danced All Night"

Sung by Marni Nixon, written by Frederick Loewe

From *My Fair Lady,* produced in 1964 by Jack L. Warner for CB

Written by Alan Jay Lerner

Based on the play *Pygmalion,* by George Bernard Shaw

Directed by George Cukor

"The Sound of Music"

Sung by Julie Andrews, written by Richard Rodgers and Oscar Hammerstein II

From *The Sound of Music,* produced in 1965 by Robert Wise for TCF

Written by Ernest Lehman from the play by Howard Lindsay and Russel Crouse

Directed by Robert Wise

Musical direction by Irwin Kostal

"Where Is Love?"

Sung by Mark Lester, written by Lionel Bart

From *Oliver!,* produced in 1968 by John Woolf for Columbia

Written by Vernon Harris from the play by Lionel Bart

Based on the novel *Oliver Twist,* by Charles Dickens

Directed by Carol Reed

Musical direction by John Green

Further Listening

"The Continental," sung by Fred Astaire and Ginger Rogers. Written by Con Conrad and Herb Magidson (*The Gay Divorcee,* RKO, 1934).

"Cheek to Cheek," sung by Fred Astaire. Written by Irving Berlin (*Top Hat,* RKO, 1935).

"Give My Regards to Broadway," sung by James Cagney. Written by George M. Cohan (*Yankee Doodle Dandy,* Warner Brothers, 1942).

"White Christmas," sung by Bing Crosby. Written by Irving Berlin (*Holiday Inn,* Paramount, 1942).

"Ain't Misbehavin'," sung by Fats Waller. Written by Andy Razaf, Fats Waller, and Harry Brooks (*Stormy Weather,* Twentieth Century-Fox, 1943).

"The Trolley Song," sung by Judy Garland. Written by Ralph Blane and Hugh Martin (*Meet Me in St. Louis,* MGM, 1944).

"I Got Rhythm," sung by Gene Kelly. Written by George and Ira Gershwin (*An American in Paris,* MGM, 1951).

"Luck Be a Lady Tonight," sung by Frank Sinatra. Written by Frank Loesser (*Guys and Dolls,* Samuel Goldwyn Productions, 1955).

"The Lady Is a Tramp," sung by Frank Sinatra. Written by Jerry Leiber and Mike Stoller (*Jailhouse Rock,* MGM/UA, 1957).

"Whatever Lola Wants," sung by Gwen Verdon. Written by Richard Adler and Jerry Ross (*Damn Yankees,* Warner Brothers, 1958).

"Summertime," sung by Diahann Carroll and chorus. Written by George Gershwin (*Porgy and Bess,* Samuel Goldwyn Productions, 1959).

"Everything's Coming Up Roses," sung by Rosalind Russell. Written by Jule Styne and Stephen Sondheim (*Gypsy,* Warner Brothers, 1962).

"Hey Big Spender," sung by Shirley Maclaine. Written by Cy Coleman and Dorothy Fields (*Sweet Charity,* Universal, 1969).

"If I Were a Rich Man," sung by Topol. Written by Jerry Bock and Sheldon Harnick (*Fiddler on the Roof,* Mirisch Production Company, 1971).

"Money, Money, Money," sung by Joel Grey and Liza Minelli. Written by John Kander and Fred Ebb (*Cabaret,* Twentieth Century-Fox, 1972).

"Hair," sung by Treat Williams and chorus. Written by Gerome Ragni and James Rado (*Hair,* CIP Film Productions, 1979).

"Tomorrow," sung by Aileen Quinn. Written by Charles Strouse and Martin Charnin (*Annie,* Columbia Pictures, 1982).

"Mean Green Mother from Outer Space," sung by Levi Stubbs. Written by Howard Ashman and Alan Menken (*Little Shop of Horrors,* The Geffen Company, 1986).

Photography & Illustration Credits

Index